BEGINNER VIOLIN THEORY FOR CHILDREN

BOOK ONE

BY
MELANIE SMITH

D1546602

1 2 3 4 5 6 7 8 9 0

Visit us on the Web at www.melbay.com — E-mail us at email@melbay.com

FOREWORD

In creating this workbook, I have relied on my educational experience and many years of violin as a basis for this style of instruction. With a degree in psychology and an emphasis on early childhood development, I have used techniques to teach children effectively while still keeping it fun — the major emphasis of learning violin at an early age. This book is designed to teach theory at a level that is attainable, yet challenging. It is intended to build confidence and solidify the relationship between theory and playing. It is written so it can be used to teach beginners the basics of theory, or even to refresh musicians who might need a small review. No matter who uses this book, it will give a strong foundation to violin and, through this understanding, will foster a greater love of playing.

TABLE OF CONTENTS

THE INSTRUMENT AND BOW

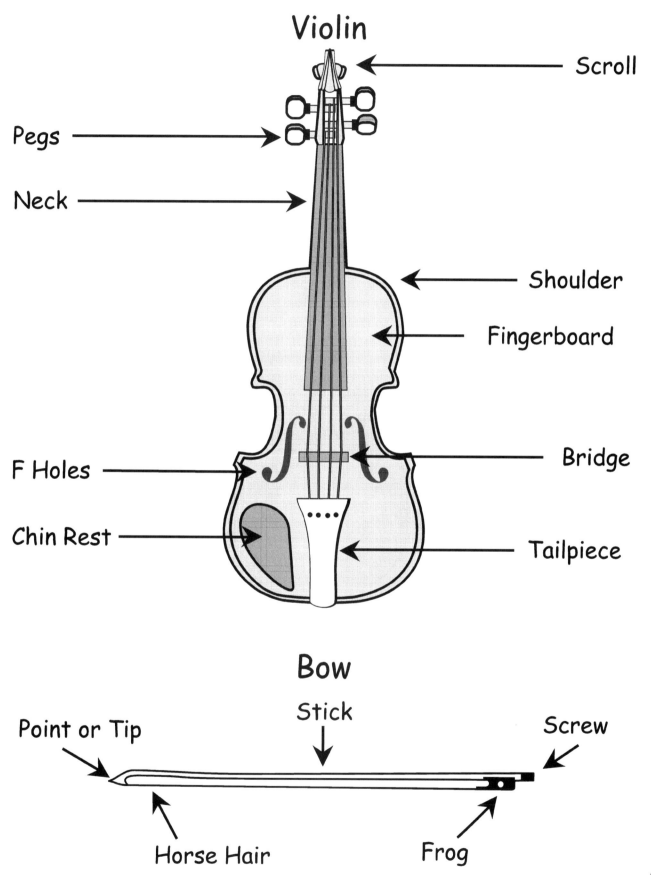

Violin

Scroll

Pegs

Neck

Shoulder

Fingerboard

Bridge

F Holes

Chin Rest

Tailpiece

Bow

Stick

Point or Tip

Screw

Horse Hair

Frog

THE INSTRUMENT AND BOW

Violin

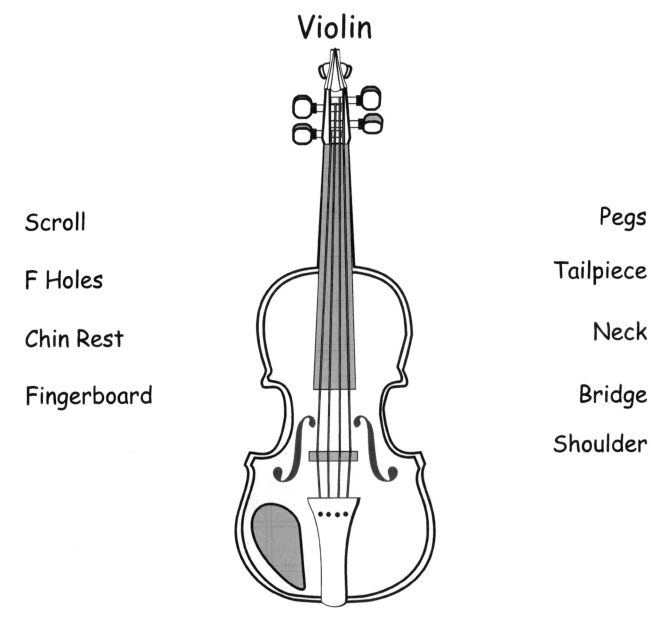

Scroll

F Holes

Chin Rest

Fingerboard

Pegs

Tailpiece

Neck

Bridge

Shoulder

Draw a line from each word
to the correct part of the violin

Stick

Point or Tip

Frog

Screw

Horse Hair

Bow

VIOLIN

How many strings does the violin have?

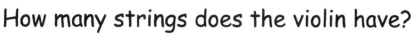

THE MUSIC STAFF

This is a music staff. It is used to tell musicians what notes to play. Notice it has 4 spaces.

Space 4
Space 3
Space 2
Space 1

Notice it has 5 lines.

Line 5
Line 4
Line 3
Line 2
Line 1

In this book we will be drawing and reading both space and line notes. It is important to know what these are.
Refer to this page if you have any questions.

DRAWING NOTES

Trace these notes very neatly in the spaces, then colour them in. Try not to trace outside the lines.

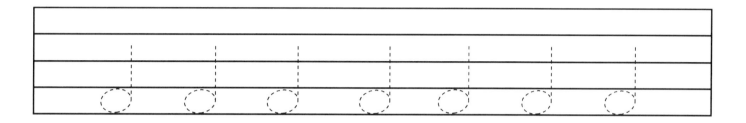

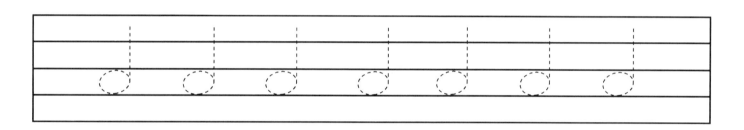

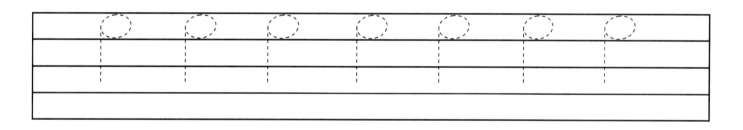

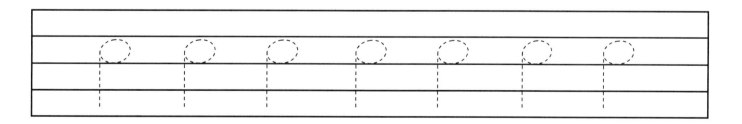

Trace these notes very neatly over the line. Make sure the line is in the middle of the circle. Colour the notes in when you are done.

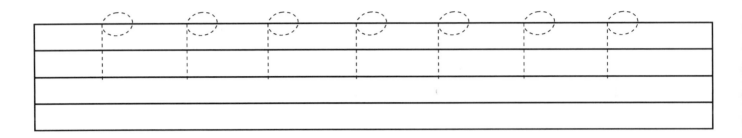

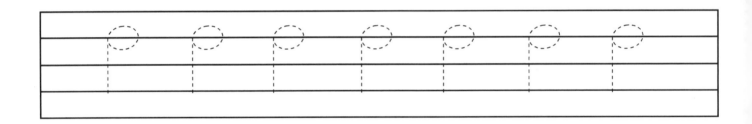

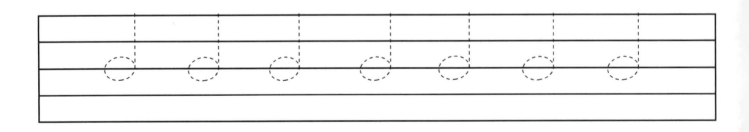

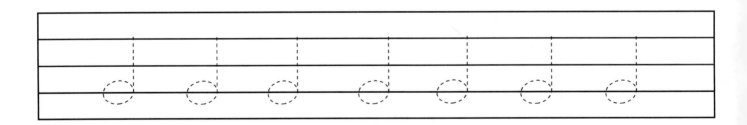

Let's mix the notes up! Trace the notes on the lines and spaces, then colour them in!

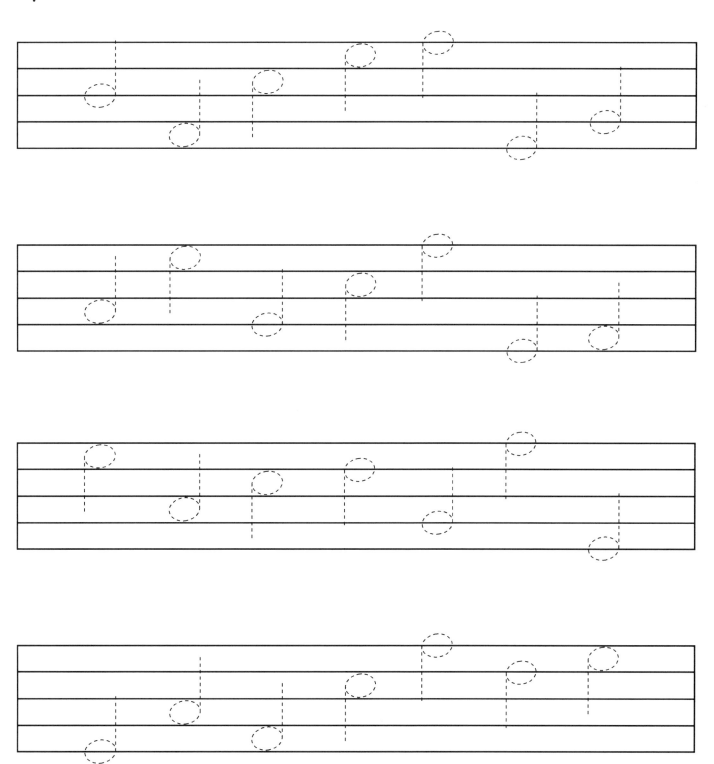

LEARNING ABOUT SPACE NOTES

Now we'll learn what a space note is. We have 4 spaces and there is a note in every space. Try counting them.

Colour the 4 space notes in!

Colour the space notes in one more time!

Draw the space notes in the four spaces by yourself.
Colour them in when you are done.

12

Draw the 4 space notes in the four spaces below, just like you did on the previous page. Remember to colour them in.

4 →
3 →
2 →
1 →

4 →
3 →
2 →
1 →

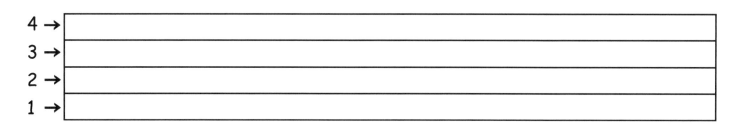

4 →
3 →
2 →
1 →

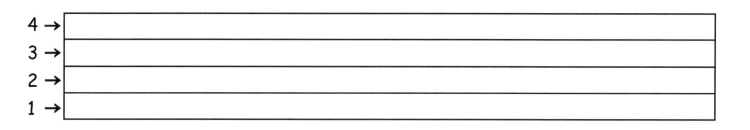

4 →
3 →
2 →
1 →

Now we will draw notes in the individual spaces.
Draw the notes you see at the beginning across the space.
Make sure the circles fit perfectly between the lines
For extra practice, colour all these notes blue.

Draw notes across in space #1.

Draw notes across in space #2.

Draw notes across in space #3.

Draw notes across in space #4.

LEARNING ABOUT LINE NOTES

We have 5 line notes.

Colour in each note.
Notice each note has a line going through the middle!

Colour in the 5 line notes one more time.

Now, try drawing these line notes on the music lines by yourself.

Start here

Draw the 5 line notes on the music lines by yourself.
Don't forget to colour them in.

Start here

Start here

Start here

Start here

Draw the 5 line notes on the individual lines. Draw the notes you see at the beginning and copy them across the line.
For extra practice, colour them in <u>yellow</u>.

Draw line notes across line #1.

5→
4→
3→
2→
1→

Draw line notes across line #5.

5→
4→
3→
2→
1→

Draw line notes across line #4.

5→
4→
3→
2→
1→

Draw line notes across line #2.

5→
4→
3→
2→
1→

Draw the notes you see at the beginning and copy them across the line, For extra practice, colour them in <u>yellow</u>.

Draw line notes across line #3.

5→
4→
3→
2→
1→

Draw line notes across line #2.

5→
4→
3→
2→
1→

Draw line notes across line #4.

5→
4→
3→
2→
1→

Draw line notes across line #1.

5→
4→
3→
2→
1→

Let's mix up the line notes and space notes. Draw circles across
the lines and spaces just like the ones you see.
Colour the line notes in yellow.
Colour the space notes in blue.

REVIEW

Colour Line notes in Red
Colour Space notes in Blue

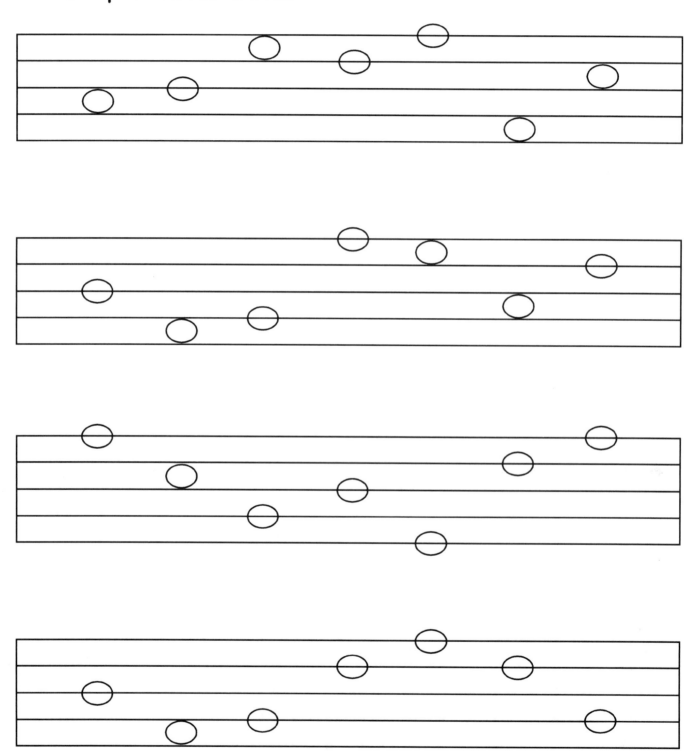

ADDING STEMS TO NOTES

Stems are the up and down lines on the sides of the notes. For this page, add stems to the notes just like the first one you see below. Make sure they are straight and touch the side of the note.

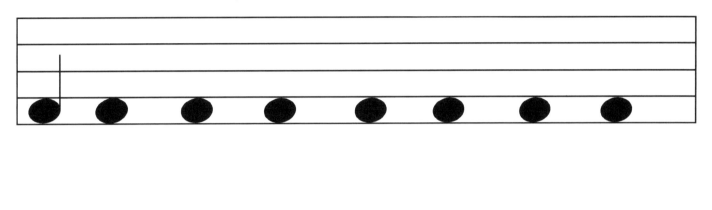

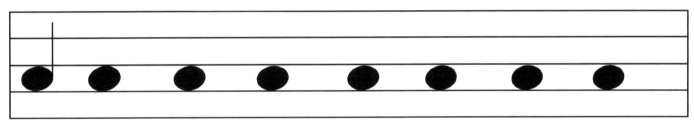

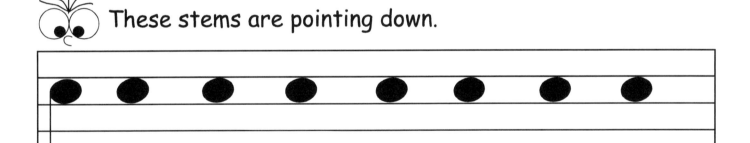

These stems are pointing down.

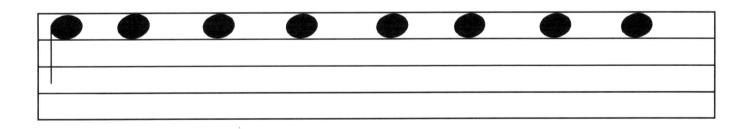

Add stems to these notes for practice. Remember these stems point up and are on the right side of the note.

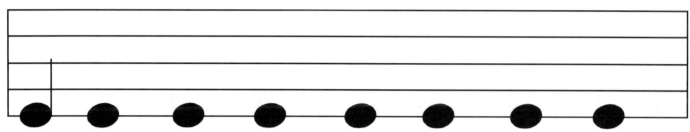

Let's add some more stems to the notes for extra practice.

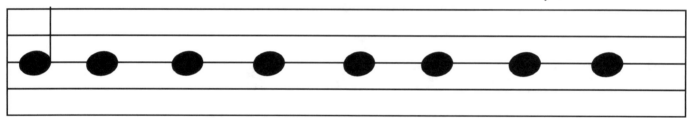

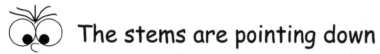 The stems are pointing down

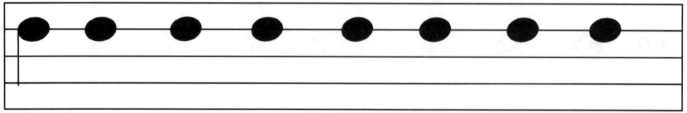

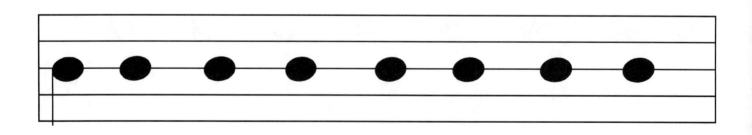

Now let's put everything we've learned together. The secret to drawing the notes with a stem up is to think of the letter d.

This note looks like a "**d**". A word with "d" is "dog"!

Draw these notes across the space by yourself

The secret to drawing the notes with a stem down is to think of the letter p. This looks like a "**p**". Let's practice drawing "p" notes.

Draw these notes across the space by yourself

DRAWING NOTES

Copy the notes exactly like the one you see.
Watch for which side of the note the stem is on.

EXCELLENT JOB!!!

REVIEW

Colour the notes with stems up in red
Colour the notes with stems down in green

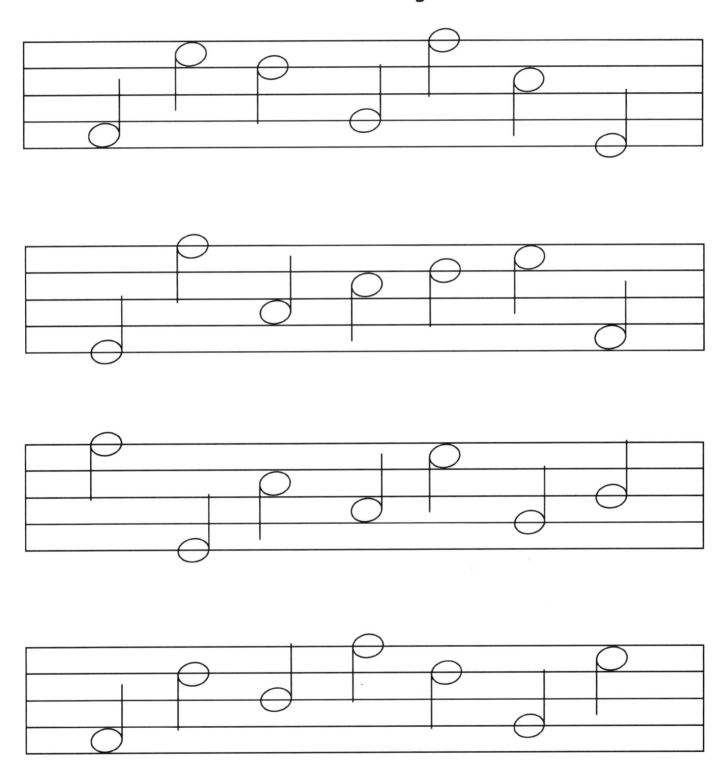

DRAWING NOTES ON LINES AND SPACES

Now we are drawing a note on every line and space starting at line 1 and going up to line 5. Look at the example below.

Now it's your turn. Start drawing every line note and space note beginning with the first note you see. Start at the bottom and put a note on every line and space.

Let's try again. Here is a example of what yours should look like.

Now draw every space and line note.

26

Draw some more notes for practice. Start from line 1 and draw a note on every line and space until you reach line 5.

Now let's add stems to these notes. Remember stems make the notes look like d's and p's. Here is an example.

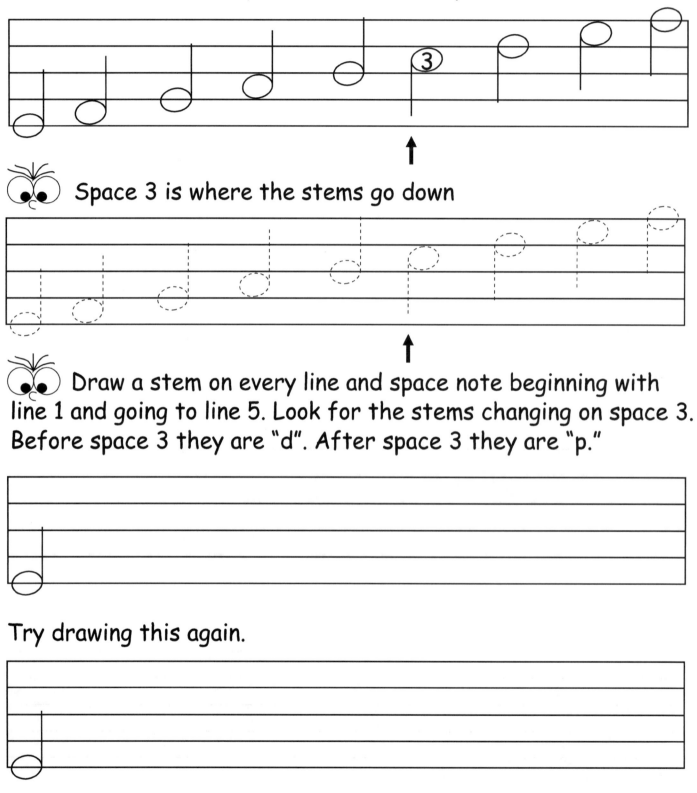

Space 3 is where the stems go down

Draw a stem on every line and space note beginning with line 1 and going to line 5. Look for the stems changing on space 3. Before space 3 they are "d". After space 3 they are "p."

Try drawing this again.

DRAWING NOTES ON LINES AND SPACES

Let's do some more for practice.
Start at line 1 and finish on line 5

Try again

Try again

Try again

LEARNING TO DRAW MUSIC SYMBOLS

I am a sharp ♯. I look like a tic tac toe. Practice tracing the sharps in this top space. Try to make them look exactly the same size. Trace the first sharp then draw the rest across the space of the sharps by yourself.

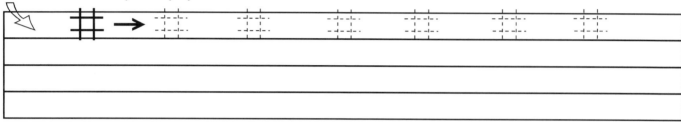

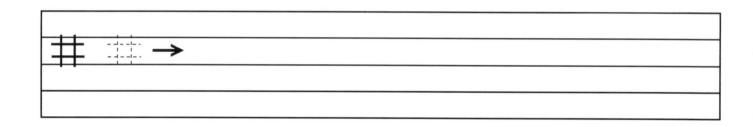

LEARNING TO DRAW MUSIC SYMBOLS

Now we will draw sharps on the lines. You should be able to see the line in the middle of the sharp

Draw across the lines.

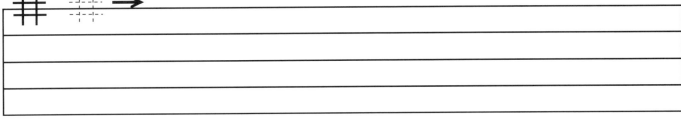

LEARNING TO DRAW NATURAL SIGNS

I am a natural sign. ♮ Think of an L and a 7, and put them together. Practice tracing naturals in the space. First trace the L, then trace the 7 for each natural.

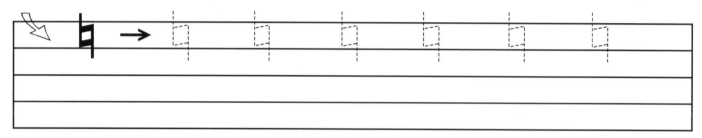

*Make sure the naturals are in the spaces and look exactly like the first one. Trace the first natural sign then draw the rest of the natural signs by yourself across the space.

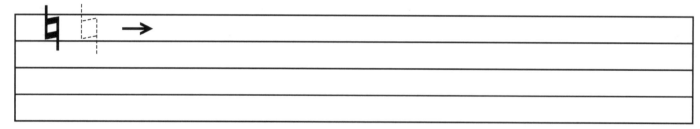

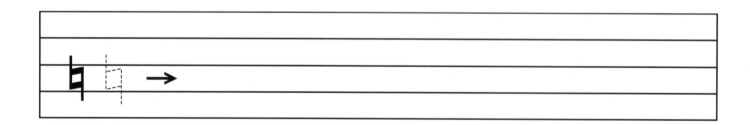

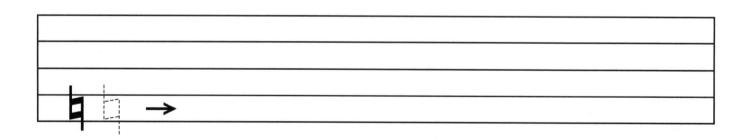

LEARNING TO DRAW NATURAL SIGNS

Now we will draw natural signs on the music lines. You should be able to see the music line in the middle of the natural sign. Remember L then 7. Trace the first natural sign then draw the rest of the natural signs by yourself on the lines.

LEARNING TO DRAW A FLAT

I am a flat. ♭ I look like a funny shaped "b". Practice tracing flats in this space.

Trace the first natural flat then draw the rest of the flats by yourself across the space.

LEARNING TO DRAW A FLAT

Let's draw flats on our music lines. Make sure the middle of the flat has the line going through it. Trace the first flat then draw the rest of the flats by yourself across the line.

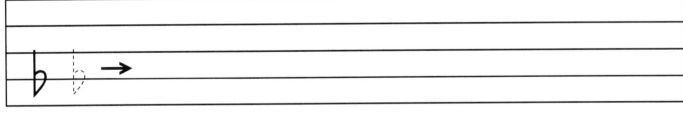

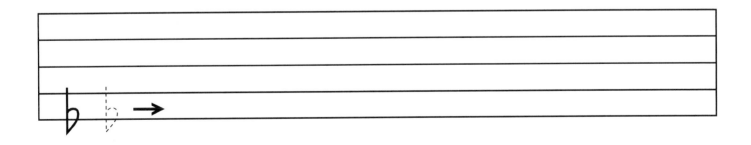

CHECKPOINT #1

Inside the boxes:

☐ Draw a note with its stem up

☐ Draw a note with its stem down

☐ Draw a sharp

☐ Draw a flat

☐ Draw a natural sign

36

DRAWING SHARPS IN FRONT OF NOTES

If we put a sharp in front of the note, that note sounds higher

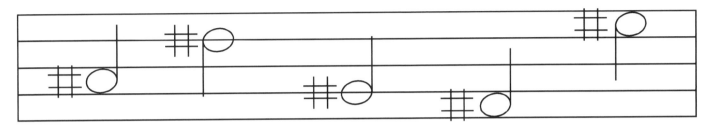

When you draw sharps in front of notes, make sure the sharp
is on the same space or line that the note is on.
Add sharps in front of these notes.

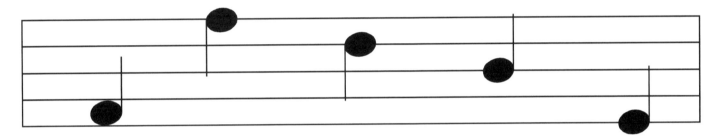

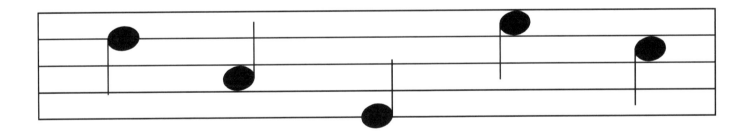

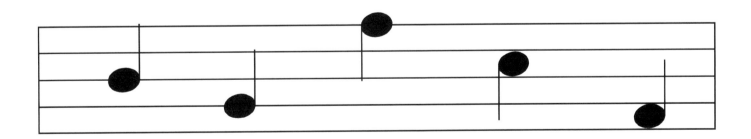

DRAWING NATURAL SIGNS IN FRONT OF NOTES

We use naturals in music to let us know if a note sounds higher or lower.

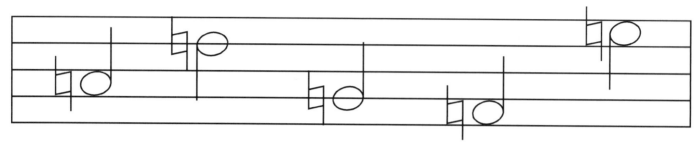

When you draw natural signs in front of notes, make sure the natural sign is on the space or line that the note is on.
Add natural signs in front of these notes.

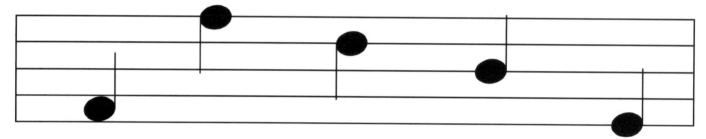

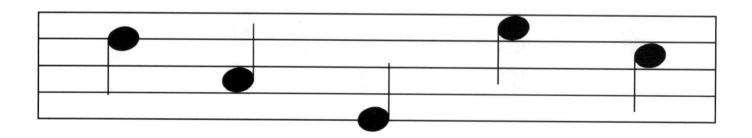

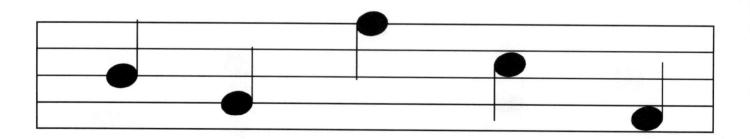

DRAWING FLATS IN FRONT OF NOTES

If we put a flat in front of a note, that note sounds lower.

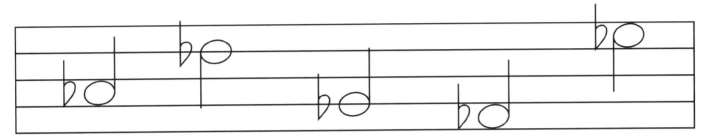

When you draw flats in front of notes, make sure the flat is on the space or line that the note is on.
Add flats in front of these notes.

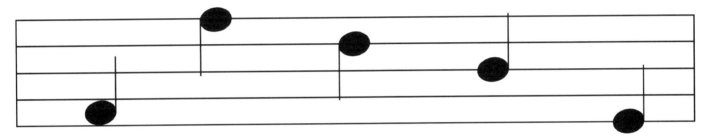

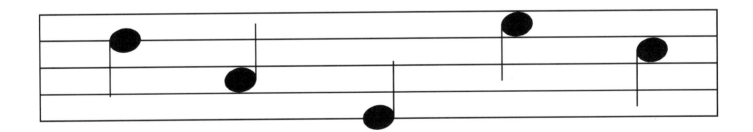

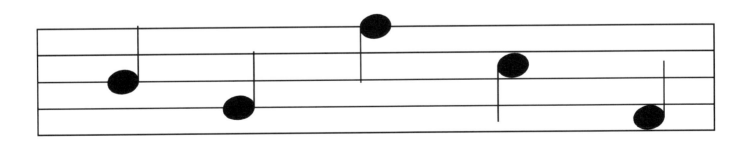

Use this page for extra practice for anything you have learned so far.

LEARNING TO DRAW TREBLE CLEFS OR G CLEFS

Now we will learn to draw treble clefs. If we see a treble clef in music, we know that the music is for the violin. For each treble clef, start at the bottom, go up to the top, move right and follow the rest of the circle.

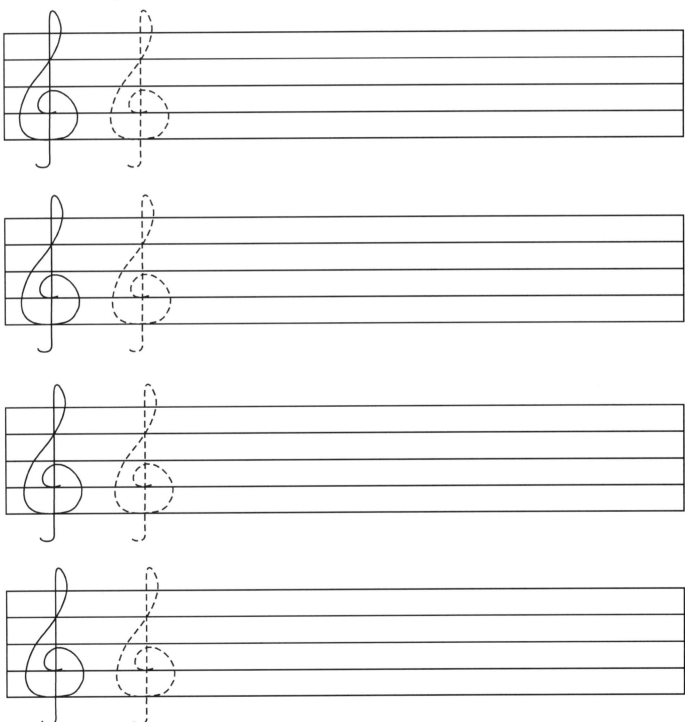

Now it's your turn. Draw the treble clefs by yourself. Start at the bottom dotted line.

LEARNING WHAT NOTES LOOK LIKE

I am a **whole note.**

I am a **half note.**

I am a **dotted half note.**

I am a **quarter note.**

I am a **eighth note.**

I am a **sixteenth note.**

Draw **whole notes** across the music staff. Make sure you look carefully to see if the note is on a line or a space.

Draw whole notes across the line

Draw whole notes across the line

Draw whole notes across the space

Now draw **<u>dotted half notes</u>** across the music staff. Make sure you look carefully to see if the note is on a line or a space.

Draw dotted half notes across the line.

Draw dotted half notes across the line.

Draw dotted half notes across the space.

Now draw **half notes** across the music staff. Make sure you look carefully to see if the note is on a line or a space.

Draw half notes across the space.

Draw half notes across the line.

Draw half notes across the line.

Now draw **<u>quarter notes</u>** across the music staff. Make sure you look carefully to see if the note is on a line or a space and each note in.

Draw quarter notes across the line.

Draw quarter notes across the line.

Draw quarter notes across the line.

Now draw **eighth notes** across the music staff.
Watch to see if the note is on a line or a space.

Remember, I have a tail ♪ and am dark in the middle.

Draw eighth notes across the space.

Draw eighth notes across the space.

Draw eighth notes across the space.

Now draw **sixteenth notes** across the music staff.
Watch to see if the note is on a line or a space.

Remember, I have 2 tails ♪ and am coloured in.

Draw sixteenth notes across the space.

Draw sixteenth notes across the space.

Draw sixteenth notes across the line.

CHECKPOINT #2

Colour the shapes with the correct colour. Look to see what symbol they have and use the guide to the right.

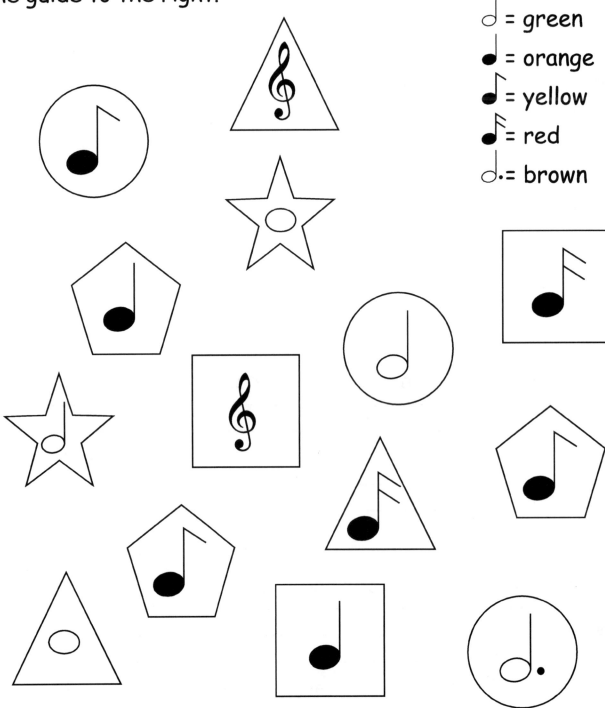

𝄞 = purple

○ = blue

𝅗𝅥 = green

♩ = orange

♪ = yellow

♬ = red

𝅗𝅥. = brown

WRITING MUSIC

Start with a Treble Clef and draw 4 whole notes on each of the 4 spaces. Remember, music always starts with a treble clef and continues with notes.

Try it again.

Try it again.

Copy exactly what is below on the blank music staff. Start with a Treble Clef and draw 5 whole notes on each of the 5 lines.

Try it again.

Try it again.

Copy exactly what is below on the blank music staff. Start with a Treble Clef and draw the half notes on each of the 4 spaces.

Make sure to change your stem from up to down.

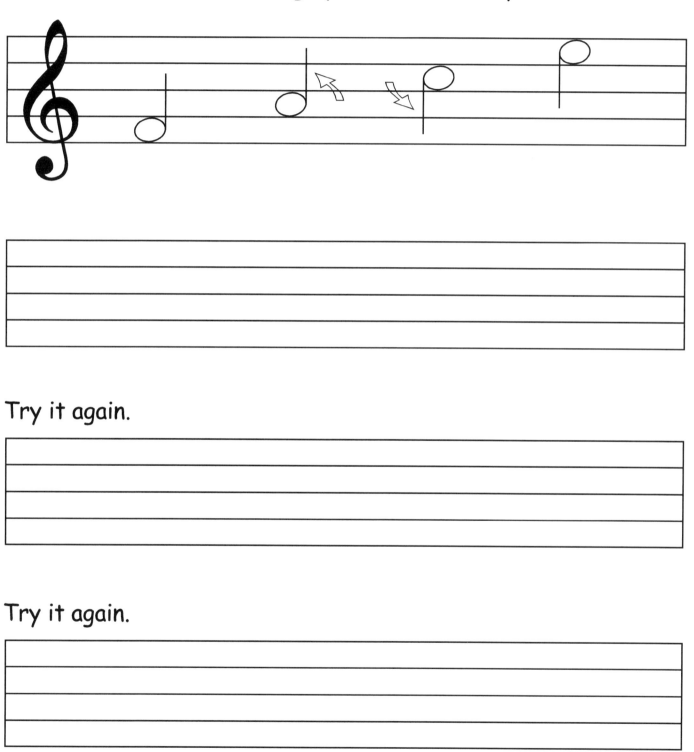

Try it again.

Try it again.

Copy exactly what is below on the blank music staff. Start with a Treble Clef and draw the 5 half notes on each of the 5 lines.

Make sure to change your stem from up to down.

Try it again.

Try it again.

Copy exactly what is below on the blank music staff. Start with a Treble Clef and draw 4 quarter notes on each of the 4 spaces.

Make sure to change your stem from up to down.

Try it again.

Try it again.

Copy exactly what is below on the blank music staff. Start with a Treble Clef and draw 5 quarter notes on each of the 5 lines.
Make sure to change your stem from up to down.

Try it again.

Try it again.

Copy exactly what is below on the blank music staff. Start with a Treble Clef and draw 4 eighth notes in each of the 4 spaces.
Don't forget to add a tail!

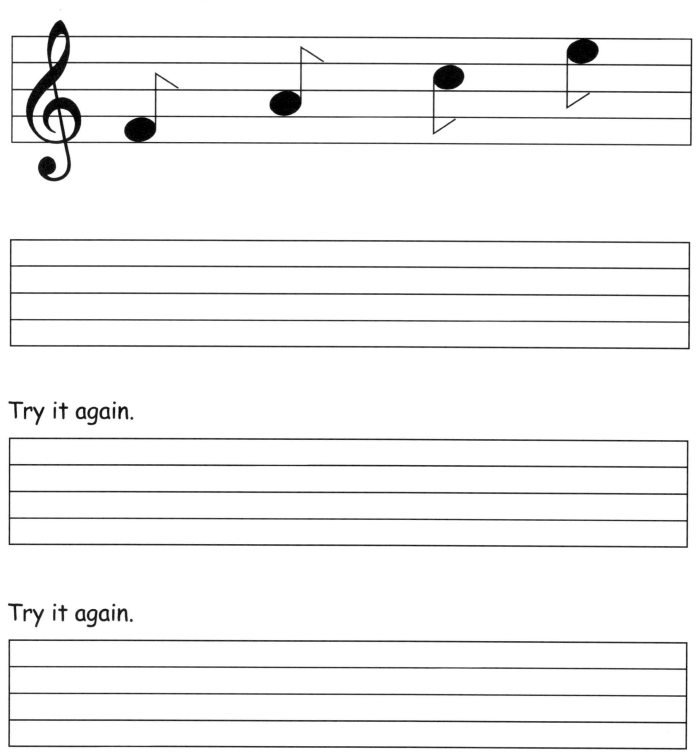

Try it again.

Try it again.

Copy exactly what is below on the blank music staff. Start with a treble clef and draw 5 eighth notes on each of the 5 lines.

 Don't forget to add a tail!

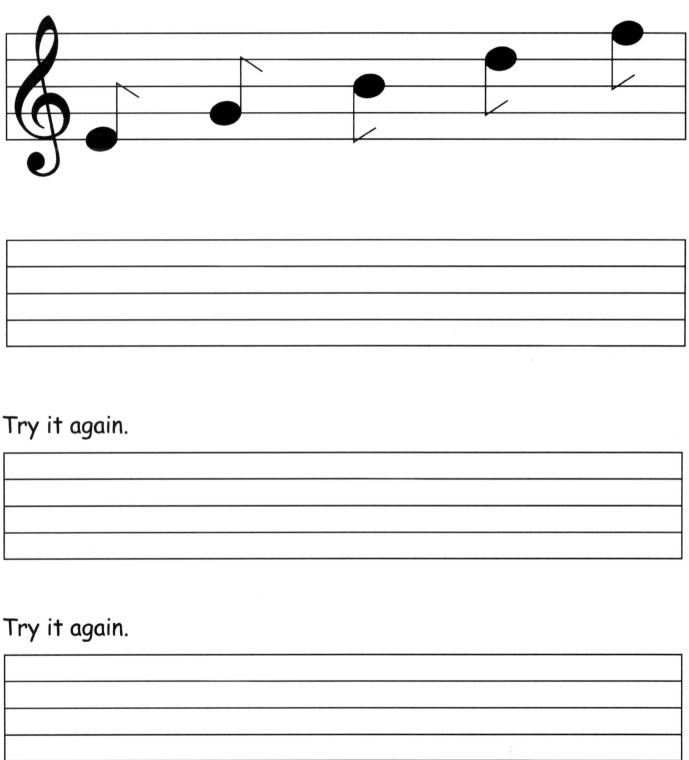

Try it again.

Try it again.

LEARNING NOTE TIMES

WHOLE NOTE

I have 4 beats!

DOTTED HALF NOTE

I have 3 beats

HALF NOTE

I have 2 beats

59

LEARNING NOTE TIMES

QUARTER NOTE

I have 1 beat

EIGHTH NOTE

I am quick.
I have ½ a beat!

SIXTEENTH NOTE

I am really quick.
I have ¼ beat!

Draw a line of **Whole Notes**. They have ___ beats each.

Draw a line of **Whole Notes**. They have ___ beats each.

Draw a line of **Half Notes**. They have ___ beats each.

Draw a line of **Half Notes**. They have ___ beats each.

Draw a line of **Dotted Half Notes**. They have ___ beats each.

Draw a line of **Dotted Half Notes**. They have ___ beats each.

Draw a line of **Quarter Notes**. They have ___ beats each.

Draw a line of **Quarter Notes**. They have ___ beats each.

Draw a line of **Eighth Notes**. They have ___ beats each.

Draw a line of **Eighth Notes**. They have ___ beats each.

Draw a line of **Sixteenth Notes**. They have ___ beats each.

Draw a line of **Sixteenth Notes**. They have ___ beats each.

LET'S REVIEW

A Whole Note gets ____ beats.

A Half Note gets ____ beats.

A Dotted Half Note gets ____ beats.

A Quarter Note gets ____ beats.

A Eighth Note gets ____ beats.

A Sixteenth Note gets ____ beats.

Draw a:

Whole Note ____

Half Note ____

Dotted Half Note ____

Quarter Note ____

Eighth Note ____

Sixteenth Note ____

How many beats does each note have?

♪ = ____ beats.

♩ = ____ beats.

𝅗𝅥 = ____ beats.

𝅝 = ____ beats.

♪ = ____ beats.

𝅗𝅥. = ____ beats.

In the box beside each note, write how many beats that note has

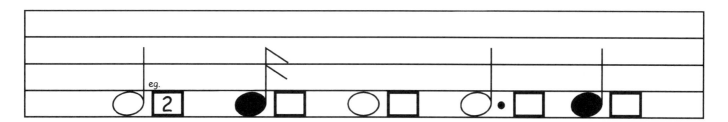

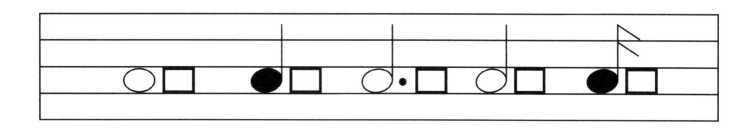

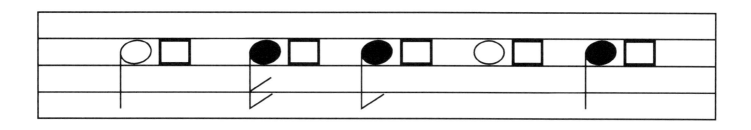

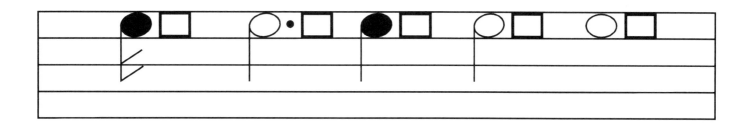

In the box beside each note, write how many beats that note has

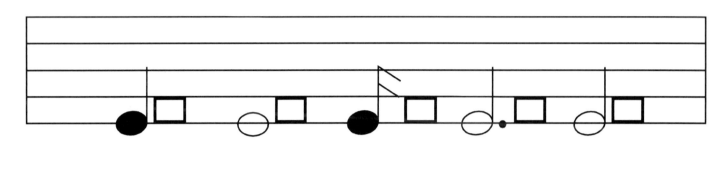

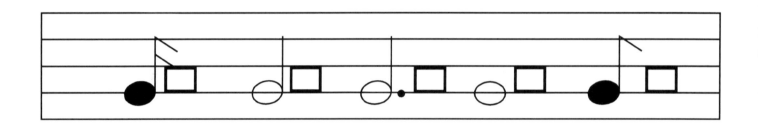

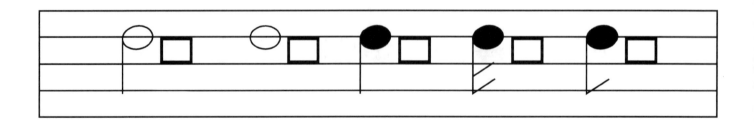

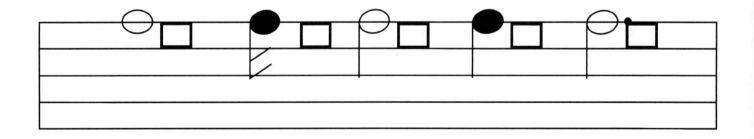

Match the following note names with the correct note drawings.

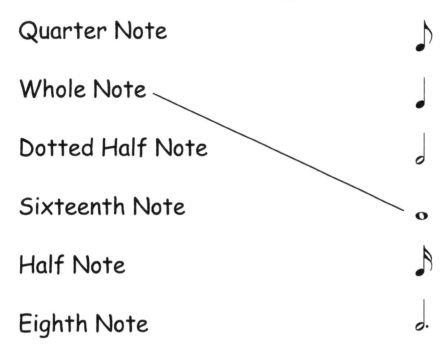

Quarter Note

Whole Note

Dotted Half Note

Sixteenth Note

Half Note

Eighth Note

Match the following note names with the correct number of beats.

Quarter Note   3

Whole Note   1/2

Dotted Half Note   1

Sixteenth Note   2

Half Note   4

Eighth Note   1/4

Match the following note times with the correct note drawings.

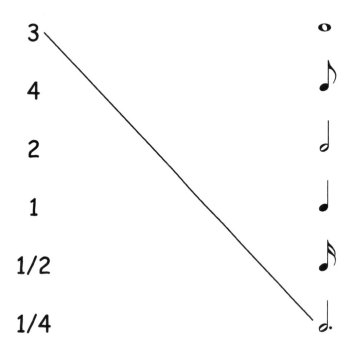

Fill in the blanks.

A _____ note has <u>4</u> beats. It looks like ○

A <u>half</u> note has <u>2</u> beats. It looks like____

A <u>quarter</u> note has _____ beats. It looks like ♩

An _____ note has <u>1/2</u> beats. It looks like ♪

A <u>sixteenth</u> note has <u>1/4</u> beats. It looks like __

A <u>dotted half</u> note has _____ beats. It looks like 𝅝.

REST VALUES

A rest is a pause where you are quiet just like a mouse.

Whole Rest

I look like an upside down hat. I have **4 beats** of quiet.

Half Rest

I look like a hat. I have **2 beats** of quiet.

Quarter Rest

I have **1 beat** of quiet.

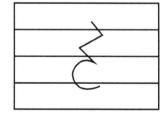

REST VALUES

Eighth Rest

I have ½ **a beat** of quiet.

Sixteenth Rest

I have a really quick quiet time. ¼ **of a beat**.

Here is an easy way to remember which is a half rest and which is a whole rest:

A half rest = ▬ = 2 beats. It looks like a hat.

A whole rest = ▬ = 4 beats. It looks like an upside down hat.

An upside down hat ▬ can fit more candy into it than a normal hat can. ▬

Draw a line of **Whole Rests.**
They look like upside down hats. They have _____ beats each.
The whole notes are below line 4

Draw a line of **Half Rests.**
They look like hats. They have _____ beats each.

Draw a line of **Quarter Rests.**
They have _____ beats each.

Draw another row of **Quarter Rests**.

Draw a line of **Eighth Rests**.
They have _____ beats each.

Draw a line of **Sixteenth Rests**.
They have _____ beats each.

LET'S REVIEW

A Whole Rest gets ___ beats.

A Half Rest gets ___ beats.

A Quarter Rest gets ___ beats.

A Eighth Rest gets ___ beats.

A Sixteenth Rest gets ___ beats.

Draw a:

Whole Rest ___

Half Rest ___

Quarter Rest ___

Eighth Rest ___

Sixteenth Rest ___

**How many beats
does each rest have?**

= ___ beats.

= ___ beats.

= ___ beats.

= ___ beats.

= ___ beats.

LET'S REVIEW

Match the following rest names with the correct drawing.

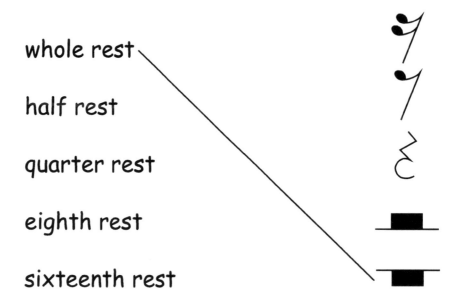

whole rest

half rest

quarter rest

eighth rest

sixteenth rest

Match the following rest names with their correct beats of quiet.

whole rest	2
half rest	1/2
quarter rest	4
eighth rest	1
sixteenth rest	1/4

LET'S REVIEW

Match the following rest time with the correct drawing.

4

2

1

1/2

1/4

Fill in the blanks.

1) A _____ rest has <u>4</u> beats. It looks like .

2) A <u>half</u> rest has <u>2</u> beats. It looks like ____.

3) A <u>quarter</u> rest has ____ beats. it looks like ____ .

4) An <u>eighth</u> rest has <u>1/2</u> a beat. It looks like ____.

5) A <u>sixteenth</u> rest has <u>1/4</u> of a beat. It looks like ____.

BIG REVIEW

Match the note with the rest of the same value.

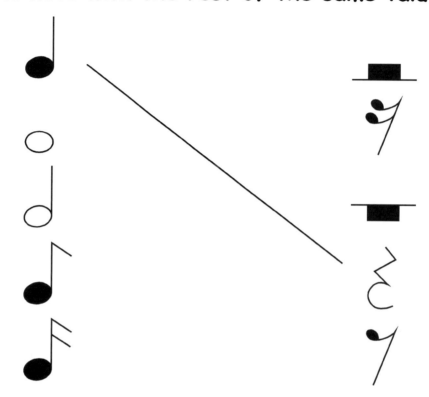

Match the note name with the rest name that has the same number of beats.

Whole Note	Half Rest
Half Note	Eighth Rest
Eighth Note	Sixteenth Rest
Sixteenth Note	Quarter Rest
Quarter Note	Whole Rest

Draw notes & rests with 4 beats in the triangles. △
Draw notes & rests with 2 beats in the squares. □
Draw notes & rests with 1 beat in the circles. ○
Draw notes & rests with 1/2 beat in the stars. ☆
Draw notes & rests with 1/4 beat in the pentagons. ⬠
Draw notes & rests with 3 beats in the rectangles. ▭

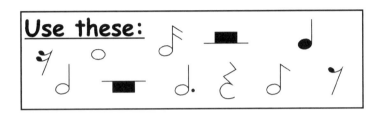

Use these:

Example:

EASY MUSIC MATH

For this page, use all the notes and rests you know. Fill in the blanks using either a note or a rest. You get to choose.
Here are the notes and rests you know:

𝅝 𝅗𝅥. 𝅗𝅥 ♩ ♪ 𝅘𝅥𝅯   𝄻 𝄺 𝄼 𝄽 𝄾

1 + 1 = 2 ♩ + 𝄽 = 𝅗𝅥	2 + 2 = 4 ___ + ___ = ___
2 + 1 = 3 ___ + ___ = ___	3 + 1 = 4 ___ + ___ = ___
1 + 3 = 4 ___ + ___	1 + 2 = 3 ___ + ___ = ___
$\frac{1}{2}$ + $\frac{1}{2}$ + 2 = 3 ___ + ___ + ___ = ___	$\frac{1}{4}$ + $\frac{1}{2}$ + $\frac{1}{4}$ + 1 = 2 ___ + ___ + ___ + ___ = ___
4 - 1 = 3 ___ - ___ = ___	4 - 2 = 2 ___ - ___ = ___

3 - 1 = 2 - =	4 - 1 = 3 - =
2 + 2 = 4 + =	4 - 2 = 2 - =
3 + 1 = 4 + =	4 - 3 = 1 - =
2 + 1 = 3 + =	3 - 1 = 2 - =
$\frac{1}{2} + \frac{1}{2} + 1 = 2$ + + =	$\frac{1}{4} + \frac{1}{2} + \frac{1}{4} = 1$ + + =
1 + 1 = 2 + =	2 - 1 = 1 - =

EASY MUSIC MATH

For this page, use the notes and rests below:

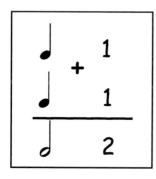

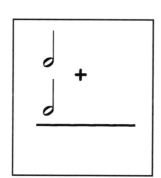

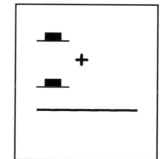

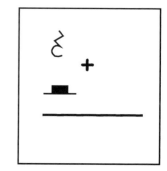

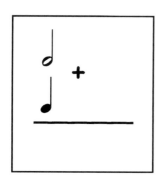

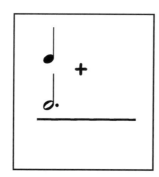

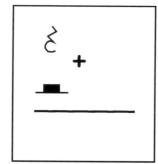

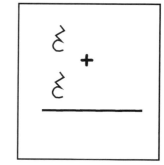

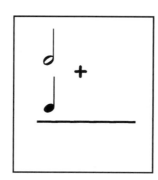

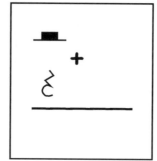

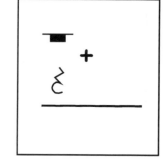

FOR OLDER CHILDREN - MUSIC MATH

Fill in the following note that makes the proper note values equal the total number of beats. 👀 It helps if you write the note beat under the note.

Use these notes to do this exercise. 𝅝 ♪ 𝅗𝅥 𝅘𝅥 ♪ 𝅗𝅥.

1) 𝅘𝅥 + 𝅗𝅥 + __𝅗𝅥.__ = 6 beats
   (1 + 2 + 3 = 6 beats)

2) 𝅗𝅥. + ____ = 5 beats

3) 𝅘𝅥 + 𝅘𝅥 + ____ = 4 beats

4) 𝅘𝅥 + ♪ + ____ = 2 beats

5) 𝅗𝅥 + ____ = 3 beats

6) 𝅝 + 𝅗𝅥 + 𝅘𝅥 + ____ = 8 beats

7) 𝅝 + 𝅝 + ____ = 9 beats

8) 𝅘𝅥 + 𝅘𝅥 + ____ = 4 beats

9) 𝅘𝅥 + ____ = 4 beats

10) ____ + 𝅗𝅥 = 5 beats

11) 𝅗𝅥. + 𝅘𝅥 + ____ = 5 beats

12) 𝅘𝅥 + ____ = 4 beats

13) 𝅗𝅥. + 𝅗𝅥. + ____ = 7 beats

14) 𝅝 + 𝅘𝅥 + ____ = 6 beats

15) 𝅘𝅥 + ____ = 3 beats

16) 𝅗𝅥 + 𝅘𝅥 + ____ = 4 beats

17) 𝅘𝅥 + 𝅗𝅥 + ____ = 5 beats

18) 𝅗𝅥 + 𝅘𝅥 + ____ = 6 beats

19) 𝅝 + 𝅘𝅥 + ____ = 7 beats

20) ♪ + ♪ + 𝅗𝅥 + ____ = 4 beats

FOR OLDER CHILDREN - MUSIC MATH

Fill in the missing rest that makes the final beat correct.
It helps if you write the rest beat number under the note.

Use these rests to do the exercise:

▬   ▬   𝄼   𝄼   𝄾

1) ▬ + ▬ = 4
    (2 + 2 = 4)

2) ▬ + ___ = 5

3) 𝄾 + 𝄾 + ___ = 3

4) 𝄼 + 𝄼 + ▬ + 𝄾 + ___ = 8

5) ▬ + ▬ + ___ = 7

6) 𝄾 + ___ = 2

7) 𝄾 + ___ = 3

8) ▬ + 𝄾 + ___ = 4

9) ▬ + ▬ + ___ = 8

10) 𝄾 + ▬ + ___ = 7

11) ▬ + ___ + 𝄼 + 𝄼 = 6

12) 𝄾 + ▬ + ___ = 5

13) ▬ + 𝄾 + ___ = 4

14) 𝄾 + ___ + 𝄾 = 3

15) 𝄾 + 𝄼 + 𝄼 + ___ = 6

16) ▬ + ▬ + ___ = 10

17) ▬ + ▬ + ___ = 7

18) 𝄾 + ▬ + 𝄾 + ___ = 6

19) ▬ + 𝄾 + ___ = 7

20) 𝄼 + 𝄼 + 𝄼 + ___ = 5

82

MELANIE SMITH

Melanie Smith has studied music since the age of three. Her training has been predominately on the violin and piano, however, she also plays the viola, cello and guitar. Throughout her violin career, Melanie studied classical, fiddle and jazz violin, as well as performed with the Edmonton Youth Orchestra, as a member of a quartet, and as a soloist.

The idea for this book arose from Melanie's experience as a violin teacher for young children. She found she needed a theory book that was specifically designed to complement violin instruction, while still allowing theory to be engaging and fun for her students.

Melanie holds a degree in Psychology from the University of Alberta, and has an After Degree in elementary education. Melanie lives in Edmonton, Alberta, Canada.

Certificate
of Accomplishment

This certifies that

_____

has successfully completed Book One
Beginner Violin Theory
for Children workbook

_____

Teacher

_____

Date